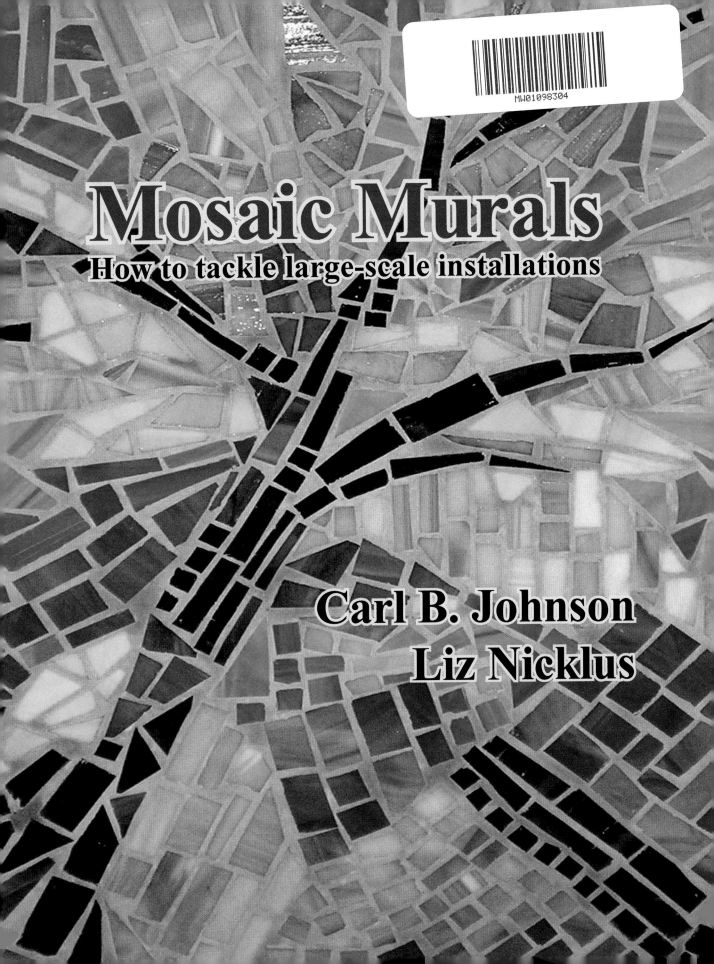

Mosaic Murals

How to tackle large-scale installations

Carl B. Johnson

Liz Nicklus

MOSAIC MURALS
How to tackle large-scale installations

Printed in the United States of America

First Printing: April 2010

ISBN: 1451548257
EAN-13: 9781451548259

Contents

Raritan Valley Community College Performing Arts Center

PREFACE AND ACKNOWLEDGMENTS

I have to acknowledge Liz, who is much more than my partner, for tempering my writing and helping me to channel it into projects that are beneficial. Liz has added her own insights and commentary to my rough draft, and has served as my editor and critic. It is she that has kept this essay on track – if left to my own devices it would certainly have derailed in any number of directions.

It is our hope that you the reader will enjoy the invitation to join our journey, and will also find helpful tips and advice for your own endeavors. This is not strictly a how-to. We write about our own challenges, and even our mistakes, for art is more than a career choice, it is a lifestyle.

Liz and I own a large library of how-to books on art in general, and on mosaics specifically. There seems to be a preponderance of guides on how to decorate vases and flowerpots, but a scarcity of books on how to tackle large-scale projects. Our goal was to provide an easy to understand guide for those enterprising souls that want to tackle a mosaic project that is bigger than a breadbox.

Carl B. Johnson
Liz Nicklus

Detail from Raritan Valley Community College Performing Arts Center

When artist Liz Nicklus took a hiatus from painting and concentrated her energies on fine art mosaics, she had little idea the direction this was going to take her art. That was almost a decade ago – her solo show at High Street Design Gallery in Millville, NJ included dozens of vases, mirrors and pots transformed by Pique Assiette mosaic.

It didn't take her long to think bigger. Liz enrolled in a workshop with famed Philadelphia mosaic artist Isaiah Zagar, and learned his techniques for covering entire sides of buildings with tile, broken ceramics, mirror and bric-a-brac.

Shortly afterward, Liz used this knowledge and began working with under-privileged kids in Millville, creating large-scale public displays in the style of Zagar. The rewards of teaching inner city children an artistic skill were manifold.

Children seem remarkably drawn to mosaics - I think it has something to do with the tactile quality and the freedom to go "outside the lines".

Children seem remarkably drawn to mosaics - I think it has something to do with the tactile quality and the freedom to go "outside the lines".

These temporary works soon became permanent fixtures in the local arts district plaza. Building on her experience, Liz quickly began to develop her own unique style, which she soon incorporated into her mixed media art. Bigger wasn't big enough, and she began contemplating large-scale architectural installations.

I am Carl B. Johnson, an abstract expressionist painter, attempting to capture and document the changing faces and disappearing places of my south Jersey home. I have delved into abstraction after being bored with objective painting, and I play around with found-object sculpture and assemblage.

I am also a writer and publisher. I founded an underground arts newspaper, INFERNO in 2002. From that literary rag I expanded into writing my own books, and co-writing and publishing books for others under the INFERNO label.

I had maintained a distance from Liz and her mosaics, careful not to step on her creative toes. We each maintain our separate studios, and while we will gladly steal good ideas from each other, we strive to maintain a certain artistic integrity in our own styles.

Together, Liz and I comprise Independent Artist Studios, specializing in architectural installations. It's been a process, and we have made some mistakes along the way. In the same manner that we work on mosaic murals together, as a team, we have written this tutorial and history. In this book we will share our experiences, good and bad, and provide some hopefully helpful advice for your own projects – or do my best to possibly scare you away from trying.

...we will share our experiences, good and bad, and provide some hopefully helpful advice for your own projects...

THE HISTORY OF MOSAIC

I am not an historian, and do not plan on writing anything extensive about the real history of mosaic, but it is important to understand that by undertaking this journey of creating large-scale mosaic installations you are partaking of an art form that spans millennia. The earliest known mosaics date back to 3000 or 4000 BC (historians disagree on the exact date, their memories are hazy that far back) to the ancient Sumerians. Uncovered in Uruk, clay cones were arranged in basic geometric patterns. I guess it could be argued that these mosaic patterns were the beginning of abstract art. The cones were embedded into columns, integral to the architecture.

It wasn't until millennia later, around 1500 BC that mosaic patterns were incorporated using various materials such as colored stones and shells. Glazed tiles were also beginning to be utilized. By this time the mosaic became more intricate, depicting scenes both religious and secular.

Wealthy Greeks from the fourth Century BC used mosaics as a floor covering. The centers were of pictorial scenes, with elaborate patterned borders, similar in design to "oriental" rugs. The Romans, going back to the fourth century BC, raised mosaics to a commercial art form. They used common designs for floors rather than original artwork.

Pergamonmuseum, Stiftmosaikfassaden des Tempels der Inanna in Uruk, selbst fotografiert, cone mosaic courtyard from Uruk in Mesopotamia 3000 B
This file is licensed under the Creative Commons Attribution ShareAlike 2.5

As Christianity conquered the world, the art form was borrowed. The cathedrals of Europe today still boast the exquisite craftsmanship of classical mosaic of purely religious themes. Byzantine mosaics were primarily iconic, depicting saints.

Early Islamic mosaics incorporated Byzantine themes, but did not have representations of people or human figures. The art of mosaics did not change considerably from this point in history until the 20th century. Mosaics remained an historical skilled craft, with little advancement in techniques or ingenuity in designs.

In the 19th century there was a revival of interest in Byzantine architecture, and with it a rebirth of interest in classical mosaic. The Art Nouveau movement brought mosaics into the modern era. Spanish artists Antoni Gaudi and Josep Maria Jujol created walls covered with waste tiles, and even specially made tiles in Güell Park.

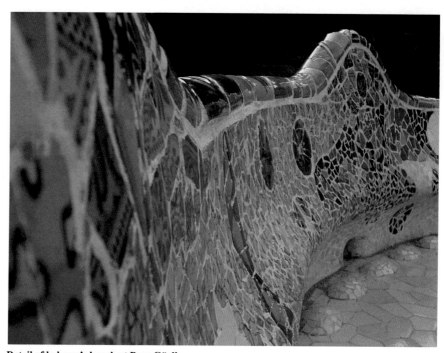

Detail of balcony's bench at Parc Güell
Taken by en:User:Burn the asylum, April 2004.
This file is licensed under the Creative Commons Attribution ShareAlike 3.0

Victorians introduced "found objects" such as shells, buttons and even toys in garden grottoes and on "putty pots". Pique Assiette began in France mid 20th century by outsider artist Raymonde Isidore. He covered his entire cottage and garden with broken pottery, and his nickname "Piqueassiette" meaning 'scrounger of cracked pots' was the genesis of a new style of mosaics.

Victorians introduced "found objects" such as shells, buttons and even toys in garden grottoes and on "putty pots".

Currently the art of mosaics is alive and flourishing. Books abound on techniques for creating mosaics on everything from flowerpots to stepping-stones, from free-form sculptures to large-scale installations. Materials range from the classic smalti and tesserae to modern mirror, cork, paper and any number of exotic materials.

For our purposes I am going to deal with only a very narrowly defined form of modern mosaics. Liz and I specialize in architectural installations. We might be caught borrowing slightly from classical forms and style, but we rely on modern materials and design. Our selection of materials is based on durability and longevity. We don't create pieces of art that will be hung on a wall, but rather installations that are integral to the surrounding environment.

8

MATERIALS - TESSARAE

In order to begin any large-scale installation, an understanding of the appropriate materials is paramount. The material list is easy. Our choice of materials to use as tesserae is an assortment of stained glass, ceramic or porcelain tile, mirror, and high-fired clay elements.

Stained Glass

Our installations are best known for our generous use of stained glass. If you are not fortunate enough to have a local supplier, or if they cannot or will not handle orders in quantities as large as you will need for a large-scale project, there are plenty of decent suppliers on the Internet. There is a compendium in the rear of this book listing trusted brands, suppliers and useful websites.

An advantage of stained glass is that it can be used in virtually any climate, and the color assortment is expansive. Stained glass doesn't fade, and it adds a depth to the mural that you just don't get with plain tile. A drawback to stained glass is that it cannot be used on floor or ground murals.

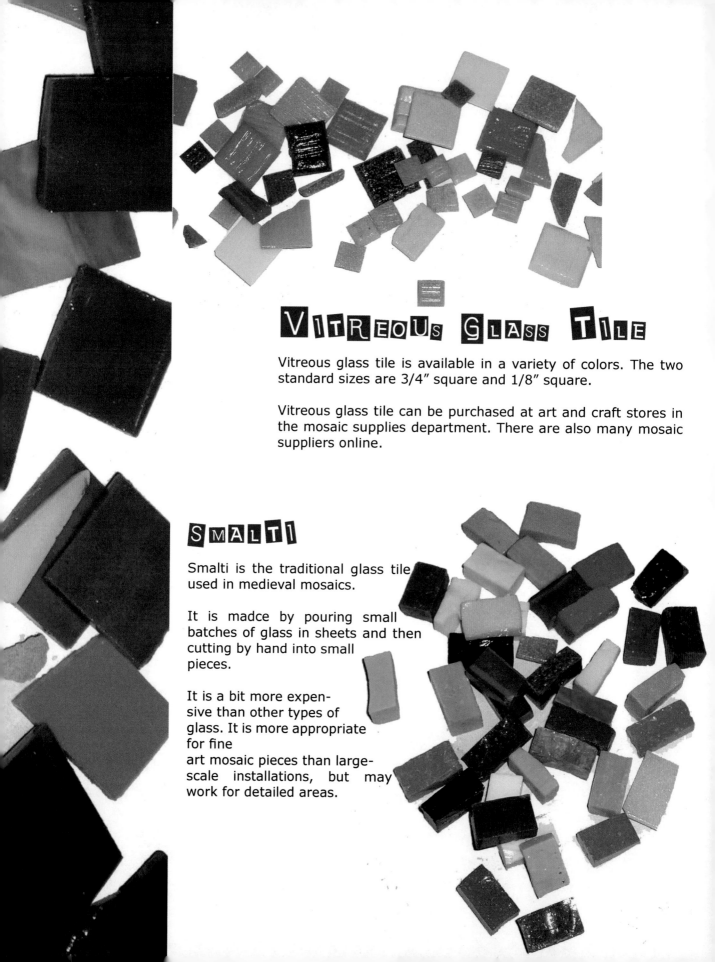

VITREOUS GLASS TILE

Vitreous glass tile is available in a variety of colors. The two standard sizes are 3/4" square and 1/8" square.

Vitreous glass tile can be purchased at art and craft stores in the mosaic supplies department. There are also many mosaic suppliers online.

SMALTI

Smalti is the traditional glass tile used in medieval mosaics.

It is madce by pouring small batches of glass in sheets and then cutting by hand into small pieces.

It is a bit more expensive than other types of glass. It is more appropriate for fine art mosaic pieces than large-scale installations, but may work for detailed areas.

SEA GLASS

Sea glass and tumbled glass are materials that look nice, but require a lot of work. Since the glass surface is porous, it stains and is very difficult to clean. It is best for exterior installations where the weather will help polish the entire mural over time.

MARBLES

An extremely affordable material that makes great highlights and accents are your run-of-the-mill marbles.

Marbles need to be pushed into a deep bed of mortar or you will risk them falling out before you get to the grouting process. You will want them embedded so that 2/3's of the marble is below the grout surface, otherwise they will pop out of the finished mural.

An alternative to children's marbles are mosaic marbles. Mosaic marbles, available from mosaic suppliers, are flattened glass spheres.

CeRAmiC ShAPED TiLEs

There is an endless assortment of novelty shaped tiles such as leaves, circles, hearts, moons and more. They add excitement and interest when used sparingly.

WHAT NOT TO USE!

You are getting the idea, by now, that the list of materials is endless. Not so!

You will not want to use any item that is made out of wood for the same reason that you wouldn't use wood as a substrate for your mural. Wood expands and contracts with the changes of humidity, and that could compromise the integrity of the bond.

Paper mache is also out for obvious reasons. Metal objects are tricky. Iron or steel will rust, and eventually stain and discolor the surface of the mural. If you really must use metal, gravitate towards aluminum or other non-ferrous metals.

Heavier objects can always be screwed into the surface prior to grouting, but as always be wary about placing objects that protrude within reach from the ground. Some people just can't resist grabbing and pulling protruding objects to see if they will hold their weight.

Tile

There are many types of tile that can be used for mosaic work. The location and type of installation will dictate the tile used. In warmer climes, you have an endless variety of tiles to choose from. Ceramic tile is perfectly suitable for the southern states. However, if you live in areas that actually have four seasons such as the great Northeast as we currently do, your choices are more limited.

While standard bathroom tile will work fine in New Mexico or Florida, most ceramic tile will absorb moisture and can crack and delaminate during the harsh freeze/thaw cycle of the northern climates.

Porcelain tile will withstand the freeze cycles, but is more expensive, harder to cut or break, and comes with a very narrow color selection.

You also have to consider the application. Is this going to be a wall installation or a pathway or floor? Ceramic tile for the floor should be rated at a minimum at Class 3 for moderate foot traffic.

Aside from the standard tiles that you would use for construction purposes, many arts and crafts supply stores carry smaller ceramic tiles designed especially for mosaic use. Not only can you buy one-inch squares in bulk but you can find a variety of fun shapes such as leaves, animals, stars, sunbursts and moons. These all can add interesting accents and focal points to an otherwise flat and potentially yawn-inspiring piece.

If you are an enterprising individual, you can find ceramic tiles from a variety of sources for cheap. Talk to your local building contractor, they will be more than happy to allow you to pick through discarded tiles from home renovation jobs. Your local tile supply store has cards and books of tile samples that are replaced or updated annually. If you have an inside person, you will soon have more tiles than you can find room to store.

Trust me, as soon as the word gets out, you will be receiving many, many types of tile, from people you don't even know. It's actually kind of nice knowing they trust you to something creative with their scraps.

And of course for exact matches you will have to hunker down and purchase cases of tile from your local retail supplier. However, if you are a loyal customer, it makes it easier to ask for the freebies such as remnants from their discard bin!

MIRRoR

A word about mirror – I have mixed feelings on mirror. It can look really good, or really gauche. I have seen amazing works done entirely in mirror. It all depends on the visual effect that you are trying to get. A universal problem with all mirror is that the silver on the back may eventually react with oxygen in the air and lime in the mortar, and the moisture and begin to turn black.

There are products available to guard against this, but none that I have seen that are 100% effective. So you have a trade-off. We have used an acrylic spray product that is applied to the back surface of the mirror, after it has been cut, with moderate success. Trust me, this is a tedious process, especially if you are working with small pieces.

Never break a mirror with a hammer, always cut mirror with a glass cutter. Besides 7-years bad luck, you will end up with shards of glass, not usable tiles.

14

RIVER ROCKS

River rocks are available at many art and craft supply stores. They add a nice natural element to any mural, and are ideal for interior or exterior installations. They will also work well for floor or ground projects.

Note: many rocks have a porous surface and are extremely difficult to clean. Use a clear flat urethane spray paint to coat the stones before use to make clean-up easier.

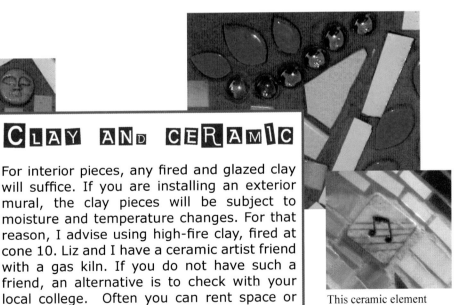

CLAY AND CERAMIC

For interior pieces, any fired and glazed clay will suffice. If you are installing an exterior mural, the clay pieces will be subject to moisture and temperature changes. For that reason, I advise using high-fire clay, fired at cone 10. Liz and I have a ceramic artist friend with a gas kiln. If you do not have such a friend, an alternative is to check with your local college. Often you can rent space or time on their kilns.

This ceramic element was designed and made by a student from the Raritan Valley Community College.

Collectible plates? Not any more when Liz wields her mighty hammer!

PLATES, BOTTLES, DETRITUS

If you plan to work in the Pique Assiette style, a whole world of materials opens to you. Cola bottles, broken china, plastic doll heads – it is only your imagination that limits you. However, in selecting materials, the same rules of temperature change and weather conditions apply. Ceramic plates will have a tendency to delaminate and crack when subjected to the freeze-thaw cycles. Certain plastics might not stick to mortar and will have to be otherwise secured.

A word to those doing art that will be permanently displayed in a public setting – have care when putting in objects that protrude from 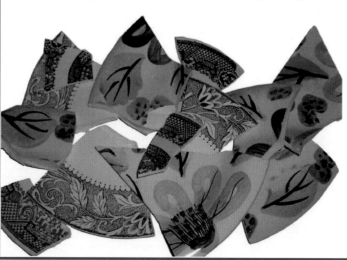 the design at ground level. Some individuals cannot resist the temptation to hang off them and see if the protruding pieces can withstand their weight. (They usually can't, which will leave a big hole in your piece).

MATERIALS AND SUPPLIES

- INSTALLATION

For interior installations, regular tile mastic is used to stick the tesserae, and sanded grout to finish the installation. For exterior installations, thin-set mortar is used to both adhere and grout.

For the purpose of this book, we will use the term "adhesive" when referring to the product used to adhere the tiles to the surface. For interior installations this will generally be tile mastic; for exterior installations it will be thin-set mortar.

We will use the term "grout" to refer to the material used to fill in the gaps of the tiles whether we are using tile grout for an indoor job, or thin-set mortar for outdoors.

There you go; you are now ready to begin your project. Get back to me and let me know how it turned out.

Okay, so you aren't ready yet. We still have to discuss tools, their use and misuse.

Tools and Supplies

At the end of this book we have included appendices with useful information. One appendix contains our mosaic mural checklist. This list contains general items that we use. Modify the list according to your own project. In the following chapters we will describe some of the common tools, their purpose, and their use.

SAFETY TIP!

Throughout this manual I will include some common sense safety tips. You want as little of your own DNA in your projects as possible. Glass and tile will slice you like a razor, something that most people want to avoid at all costs

Hammer

When we use tile our method depends on the arbitrary patterns caused by simply shattering the tile. You notice we said "tile" – NEVER try to shatter mirror or glass with a hammer. Always cut with a glasscutter, as described later in this chapter. The process is easy and therapeutic, and so easy that even a cave man could do it.

SAFETY TIP!

Put on your safety glasses! Designing a mural becomes much more difficult if you have blinded yourself with shards of tile in your eyes.

After donning your eye protection, take a tile, wrap it or cover it with a heavy rag, and give it a solid whack with a hammer.

SAFETY TIP!

Be careful when handling cut or broken tile. Tile edges can be razor sharp. It is best practice to wear heavy work gloves, one slip and you can lay your hands wide open.

TILE
CUTTERS

There are a number of basic tools for making more precision breaks on tile. For our purposes we will not go into tile saws and tools designed for making exact cuts. We are not into precision for our style mosaic, preferring instead the visual excitement of unexpected curves and breaks.

Tile Cutters are a pair of pliers with a round cutting blade on one or both jaws. To use the cutters or the nippers, again don your eye protection. This cannot be stressed too much. Shards of tile will fly in unpredictable arcs.

Wearing protective gloves, grasp the tile with one hand and place the cutter blades at the edge of the tile near where you want to make a straight break, and firmly squeeze. In most cases the tile will split cleanly and along a straight line.

There are also inexpensive tile cutters for making straight cuts. They have a scoring blade on a movable handle – you score and snap. They are generally used for tile installations where a power tile saw is too much, and nippers or cutters are too inexact. I caution you against getting too analytical – when in doubt use the hammer or select a different piece of tile.

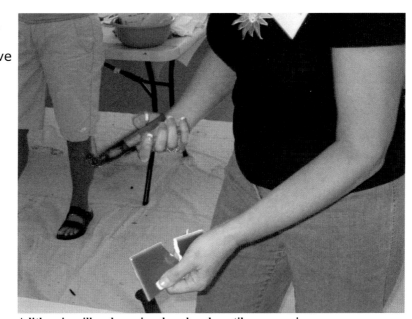

A litle snip will make a nice clean break on tile or ceramic

Tile Nippers

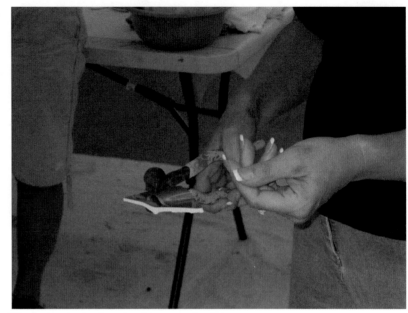

Liz demonstrates how to nip a ceramic plate.

Sometimes you may need to nip away a corner, or nip a tile to fit into an odd shaped space. For this we use the nippers. Tile nippers look like a sideways wire cutter. The jaws have wide sharpened blades. Using the nippers, make small bites along the area that you want to remove, taking off a little at a time.

Note: you should be holding the nippers in one hand and holding your tile with the other. We have seen countless beginners hold the nippers with both hands – when you do this, you have no control over the break, AND, you risk shards flying all over the place and injuring yourself or someone else.

Utilizing a little patience and self-control you can nip tiles into virtually any shape you desire.

HOW WE MAKE THE GLASS TILE

How do we get the thousands of small glass tiles we use? We make them. Whenever possible we try to buy locally. We are advocates of supporting your local economy. They provide local jobs, and pay local taxes. If you don't support your local businesses, who will? However, if you do not have a local source of glass, there are some reliable sources on the Internet. We supply a list of some of our favorites in the appendix.

We purchase the glass in sheets of 12" x 12" or 18" x 18" or even in sheets of 12" x 24". We use basic glasscutters to cut it down to size. My big sister used to do that to me.

Chances are you will not be making any compound cuts, or intricate curves. We are not creating leaded stained glass crafts. We want simple squares, rectangles and triangles. For this process a basic wheel cutter, one where you score and break, will suffice.

Since we are cutting hundreds of sheets of glass into small pieces, a cutter with a large handle will go a long way towards preventing nasty cramps in your hand.

We purchase stained glass in sheets and cut it down into tiles.

Pistol grip cutters with a built-in reservoir for cutting oil cost around $30, and may be found on on-line auction sites for much less. They are well worth the investment. If you opt for the standard glasscutters, remember to frequently dip them in a jar of turpentine or cutting oil.

Basic Glass Cutter

The large handle is easy on the hands, and serves as a reservoir for the cutting oil.

CUTTING GLASS

SAFETY TIP!
Always wear gloves when cutting and handling glass. Heavy cotton garden gloves or leather work-gloves will do the trick, and protect you from the inevitable slices that will occur when handling glass.

Lay the sheet out on a flat sturdy surface. Use a metal straight edge such as a yardstick and score the glass. You apply only enough pressure until you hear a slight dragging sound, and score the glass in a fluid, steady motion. You do this one time, do not go over the same line more than once.

SAFETY TIP!
Never, ever allow a sheet of glass to extend beyond the edge of your work surface. It just takes one moment of preoccupation, and you brush your hip or thigh against the table. It will slice you deep and can ruin your entire day.

Also, when carrying a sheet of glass, always hold the sheet vertically in front of you with your gloved hands on either side (right and left, not front and back). This way if you lose your grip and the sheet slips, it will fall in front of you and not slice up your hands.

After scoring the sheet both vertically and horizontally, creating a checkerboard pattern, tap the score marks lightly with the metal end of the glasscutter or with another metal tool.

Use running pliers to break glass after scoring with a glass cutter

Place the straight edge under the score mark, and press gently. The glass should easily fracture the entire length with a clean break. With some stained glass, especially antique glass or glass with wavy uneven surfaces you don't always get a clean break. No sweat, there are no wrong pieces. Odd-shaped tiles add excitement to the overall pattern.

A handy tool to have is a pair of running pliers. Running pliers have wide jaws that are slightly curved in an arc. A slight snap at the edge of the score will make any cut easy. It is often easier to use the running pliers for the long breaks. Most running pliers have a screw adjustment that prevents the jaws from closing all of the way. Adjust this screw so that the pliers close just a tad shy of the thickness of the glass sheet to prevent unwanted chipping on the edges.

Notice that Liz is obeying the safety rule and wearing gloves when handling glass. Also notice that she is not abiding by the other safety rule that says to never allow glass to protrude over the edge of the work table.

One firm score of the glass cutter is all it takes to make a clean cut.

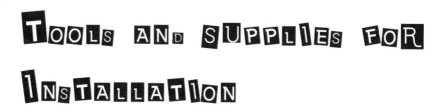

Tools and Supplies for Installation

In addition to these basic cutting tools, you will need tools and supplies for mixing and applying mortar and grout. You can never have too many plastic containers.

For large outdoor projects we use 5-gallon paint containers to mix mortar, using a large metal putty knife or trowel to mix. Smaller paint buckets that hold a quart or so, sold at most paint departments, are ideal for smaller quantities. If you are working with very small tile, paper plates and bowls are ideal and cheap.

Plastic putty knives are inexpensive and disposable. Buy them by the dozen.

For applying adhesive we use various notched trowels, plastic putty knives (buy them by the dozen, they are cheap and wear out fast) and even plastic dinner knives.

A standard tile float is used to apply grout to the finished mural.

For grouting, Liz and I have different approaches. She prefers to use the large sponges you buy in the automotive department for washing your car. I prefer the standard float.

Liz works the grout into the crevices using a sponge. This method is ideal if you have a lot of three dimensional objects set into the adhesive. A grout float works best on flat, even surfaces. If you have intricate pieces embedded into your design, you can also use your gloved fingers to push grout in and around the object.

Cut large sponges in half.

24

Gloves – besides heavy canvas or leather gloves worn while cutting the tiles, you will want to have plenty of latex or vinyl gloves. Mortar is heavy with lime content, and it will destroy your hands. If you have small cuts on your hands, you will know it right away if you attempt to mortar without gloves.

Rags – don't throw away that old tee shirt! The same goes for your worn out kitchen towels, wash cloths, and sweatshirts. You will go through a lot of rags polishing the tile.

In addition, it is good to have canvas and plastic drop cloths, and plenty of masking tape. Single edged razor blades are ideal for cleaning the tile of renegade grout during the final stages of cleaning and polishing. Another good tool is a plain old toothbrush – great for

Single-edged razor blades are ideal for cleaning up stray mortar on the finished mural.

getting grout or mortar out of little cracks and crevices.

Finally – make sure you have a first aid kit on hand. We have added one item in our kit that you would not generally consider – super glue. A drop of super glue into a fresh slice – AFTER you have cleansed the wound – will act like an instant suture and staunch the flow of blood. This is NOT an alternative to a trip to the emergency room for severe lacerations – this is just a makeshift quick fix to stop that irritating constant dripping of blood from superficial slices, the sort that seem to never stop bleeding. As stated earlier, the point is to get as little of our own DNA in the project as possible.

This just about covers the tools and supplies that you will need. We will now discuss the actual installation of murals in a step-by-step tutorial, with commentary and examples that will explain the differences between interior and exterior jobs as well as the similarities. Once you learn how to do one, you can do the other.

Detail of "Inspiration", Gloucester County Health Department, Sewel, NJ

THE BORING STUFF - METHODS

There are two basic methods of applying the tesserae, the Direct Method and the Indirect Method. (Actually each method can be divided further into more sub-methods – but you didn't buy this book to be bored with sordid details.)

Our technique lends itself to the Direct Method, the tiles, or tesserae, are adhered to the mural surface directly prior to being grouted in place.

The Indirect Method has the tiles being placed onto a backing paper, face down. The Double Indirect Method – okay so I lied and am going to bore you with details – has the tiles stuck face-up on a backing paper or mesh. Both indirect methods allow the design to be completed off-site, and applied in large sheets. This is ideal for intricate designs and detailed work. It doesn't translate well when creating pique assiette, or for our own unique style.

Sheets of glass tile that you purchase at your local building supply store are a commercially available example of double-indirect tile.

You simply apply adhesive to the surface, and lay the entire sheet comprised of smaller tile into the adhesive. Instead of applying 144 one-inch squares of glass you are laying down one 1-foot square sheet.

Tнε PʀεpαʀαΤιΟΝ

I am assuming that you will want your project to last more than a week before tiles begin crumbling off of the surface. Surface preparation is everything, especially for projects that will be subject to extreme weather conditions.

If you reside in the southern climes, you may have heard the term frost line, but have never experienced it. The frost line is the depth which soil or water is expected to freeze in winter. Here in the great northeast we have to be particularly cognizant of concrete footings, sidewalks, etc. Ceramic tiles will disintegrate as the glass coating delaminates from the ceramic tile during deep freezes. This is one reason that you do not see very many ground mosaic installations in the colder climates.

Moisture is another enemy of mosaics. Moisture and freezing temperatures together are arch-villains, The Joker and Catwoman to our Batman. Use of an acrylic additive called "milk", mixed with the mortar is recommended for any exterior installation that will be subject to frost/

Measure, and measure again.

thaw cycles. The acrylic additive prevents moisture from infiltrating the mosaic, freezing and expanding, and creating havoc.

For exterior installations, the only acceptable surfaces are cement, concrete block walls, or panels of concrete backer board secured to a sturdy non-flexible framework. Under no circumstances should you use wood or composite board as a sub-surface.

For any concrete or cement application, the surface should be sealed with a waterproof membrane. This prevents moisture from getting between the tiles and the surface causing damage, and is easily applied with a roller or brush.

A Blank Canvas

For interior installations, any firm surface such as modern sheetrock, cement board or a secure plaster wall will suffice. There are modern products that will allow you to tile over plastic laminate, and even over existing tile walls or counters. The advice we give can be carried over for smaller projects.

I am getting near the end of the boring stuff, but don't despair. There is plenty more stuff to bore your socks off to be interspersed throughout.

Sheetrock is an ideal surface for interior mosaic installations

HOW I WAS DRAGGED KICKING AND SCREAMING INTO THIS VENTURE

I mentioned already that Independent Artist Studios is a partnership between Liz Nicklus and myself. It wasn't always that way. I concentrated on my painting and publishing an underground arts newspaper, Inferno. Liz was involved in creating her art, and working in a local art program, teaching community teens and under-privileged children.

Two of her projects included Isaiah Zagar-inspired outdoor mosaic murals. These projects were large in scale, and the experience emboldened her to explore larger mosaic murals. She answered an RFP (request for proposal) to install a large-scale mosaic in the lobby of a regional childbirth center. Her proposal was accepted.

She learned some important lessons on this project, such as working with the interior designers and architects. Color schemes changed once, maybe twice. The process was grueling, going back and forth between contractors and designers and the company that brokered the artists. Liz survived, and her professionalism ensured consideration for future projects.

Me? I enjoyed the free wine and hors d'oeuvres at the opening reception, but was still reluctant to even consider getting involved in the mosaic business. I had tiling experience; I tiled my bathroom shower and my utility room, and that was enough to convince me that I didn't want to be a tile setter as a profession.

The next project was located at the main entrance to the hospital, which included a meditation walk with curved sidewalk, a garden, and a wall that is sixty-seven feet long and up to 14-feet tall. The designers and architects had envisioned a mural on the wall. Better yet, they envisioned a mosaic architectural installation similar to the lobby mural at their childbirth center, only bigger. Much bigger.

"Oceans of Reflection" 10' x 67' AtlantiCare Regional Medical Center, Atlantic City, NJ

Liz suggested that I come on as an apprentice, paid a daily rate. I still resisted. This, after all, was her baby. But crunch time came, Liz had other obligations to attend, and there were still several weeks of work left.

She and I worked together completing the installation of the tiles. Then we entered the completion stage, she watching me like a hawk as I began the long, arduous, boring process of grouting. Unfortunately I was a natural on the grouting. Grouting on an exterior installation requires applying thin-set mortar mixed to the consistency of Cream of Wheat. I should explain... Cream of Wheat the way it turns out when I make it, not Cream of Wheat the way most people make it... sort of the consistency of gritty peanut butter.

The mortar is applied – I use a grout float (which I will describe later on), Liz prefers using a heavy sponge. With either method this is the easy step. Cleaning the mortar off without leaving grooves between the tile while cleaning the haze off of the surface is where the fun begins.

Imagine the movie The Karate Kid, with the little punk going "wax on, wax off" for weeks. Grouting a project this size is pretty much the same idea. Wipe the grout on. Wipe the excess off. Polish the surface a little more. Polish the surface even more. You want the tiles and glass to sparkle. You want the edges and corners sharply defined. The mortar must come to the very edges leaving no gaps or cracks for moisture to penetrate.

Is it worth it? Absolutely! Whenever Liz and I are in the vicinity of the hospital, we drive by and inspect our handiwork. Others have called the finished mural a "landmark". It certainly was a landmark in our professional careers. It was, in the words of Rick of Casablanca fame the "beginning of a beautiful friendship."

30

Wading Ever Deeper

I had dipped my toes in the waters, and now could not resist diving in headfirst. A potential job on the West Coast had presented itself, and we discussed how far we wanted to continue in this new direction. I said "full steam ahead". We would entertain every possibility.

The director of the local housing authority contacted me that spring. He was seeking artwork to be displayed in the Authority's newest project, New Jersey's first "green" affordable senior housing facility. He was thinking paintings, possibly a painted mural.

When he showed me blue prints and elevations for the space and I envisioned not paintings or painted murals, but rather a mosaic installation. After all, what better fit for a "green" building than mosaics crafted of natural materials – glass, stone, ceramic and sand?

"River Dance" is located in the The Glasstown Residence at River Park, New Jersey's first "Green" affordable senior housing building.

This indoor mural consists of three panels, each 44 inches wide by 72 inches high. Opalescent stained glass, ceramic and glass tiles, and hand-created clay elements are highlights of this mural designed to mimic the colors and lines of nature.

I eventually met with the architectural designer and exhibited photographs of the previous mural. I took her on a tour of our town, pointing out Liz's other installations and convinced her that we would be the only logical choice for the project. I am not a natural born salesman, so this was the difficult part for me. However, when you believe in something, it does make the job of selling the concept to others much easier.

The process for an interior mosaic is different than that of an exterior. In many ways it is simpler. The selection of materials is broader, as you do not have to be concerned with weather, temperature cycles, and dampness.

YOU NEED A PLAN

One aspect of the process that is similar for all installations would be the rough illustrations we use to help our clients visualize where we are going with the mural. We are often asked why we don't provide exact diagrams of the mural. Simply, we cannot. This is not a mechanical process. We don't use blueprints, or color-by-number schematics. We work out of our heads. The mural is an extension of us, just as a painting is an extension of an artist.

We will work off of basic drawings showing color schemes and the general form and design; however each hand-cut tile is set independently. We apply the tiles, and adjust colors and lines and curves as we work. The size and shape of each unique tile dictates which tile will be placed next. Color combinations, which were mere representations on paper, might not work as well when you actually place a piece of stained glass next to another on site.

We present our clients with sketches and general color relations, as well as cards with actual material samples. We create sample mosaic panels created with the selected materials and chosen color palette.

Cover Up!. Don't skimp on painter's tape, plastic drop cloths and canvas drop cloths. Dried grout and mastic are difficult to remove if ground into carpet. The cleaning process leaves a ton of dust. You want to do everything possible to contain debris, it makes clean-up easier.

From this point forward, we ask our clients to trust us. Is that too bold? We are not arrogant; we are simply confident that as practicing artists we do know what is going to work best on the finished product. And we don't think we are boasting when I claim that our clients have not been disappointed.

However, back to the prep-work. When working on-site you have to be really cognizant to avoid

A Blank Canvas. Look closely and you will see the rough magic marker lines used as guides for the design. Liz used a plastic putty knife to apply the "mud" - that is cool pro-speak for mortar - along the line and then pressed the mirrored tiles into place.

getting dust, grout, mastic, and fragments of the tile on furniture or in the carpet. Our first order of business is always to measure, and measure again. For the Housing Authority Senior Center, we had proposed three separate panels, applied directly to the sheet rock, spaced equally across the wall.

Liz and I made an on-the-spot executive decision (the architectural designer that we were working with did give us quite a bit of latitude) to move the end panels closer inward and to leave more space on either end. What seemed to work on the rough sketches did not work in the actual environment. A little trust goes a long way.

After figuring out the placement of the panels, we use blue painter's tape to mask off the perimeter of the panel(s). Then we tape plastic drop cloths around all the exposed areas to the side and below to protect the new job or surrounding surface material.

DON'T BE AFRAID TO IMPROVISE

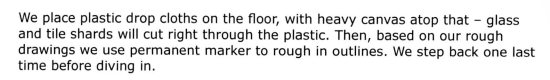

We place plastic drop cloths on the floor, with heavy canvas atop that – glass and tile shards will cut right through the plastic. Then, based on our rough drawings we use permanent marker to rough in outlines. We step back one last time before diving in.

We will then select opposite sides to commence work, and lay in the outlines. In the examples shown, we used a lot of mirror to create the divisions of color and delineate the fields. If there are ceramic elements, they are placed at this time also.

We will apply whatever border elements we are using. In some cases the border will be mirror, in others it might be ceramic cove tile to create a frame. In others, there is no specific frame; the tile is simply cut to conform to the boundary.

We begin setting the tile. The tile in most cases is stained glass purchased in 18" x 18" sheets that were painstakingly cut into tesserae at our studio workspace. This was part of the weeks of preparation work that nobody sees.

Liz is selecting and placing the ceramic elements on this interior installation.

Whether interior or exterior, the design layout is similar. Notice the ample use of masking tape to mark the boundaries. This ensures straight clean grout lines on the finished mural.

WHAT NOT TO DO!

The secret to success in the arts, as well as in many endeavors, is to volunteer. Liz and I have a difficult time saying "no" and so end up involved in a plethora of community activities.

The upside of volunteerism is that you make contacts and find opportunities that might otherwise not be available. With this in mind, we decided to create a temporary mosaic mural that would be donated to the Sculpture garden at the Noyes Museum in Oceanville, NJ.

Granted, the mural was intended to be temporary, but not as temporary as it turned out to be. This section will be a lesson in what not to do. The first thing not to do is to use wood as a subsurface for any outdoor piece.

Wood absorbs moisture, warps, expands and contracts, and stresses the grout joints as it goes through these contortions. There is no way to prevent this. We knew this, but still opted to use marine plywood as the base for this temporary installation.

While this photo may be an exaggeration, the climate and elements affect all wood in an adverse manner! Wood absorbs moisture, warps and expands and contracts. This affects the ability of mortar to adhere.
Photo courtesy of Darren Hester.

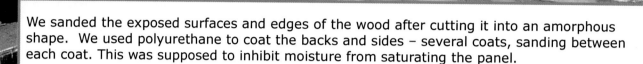

We sanded the exposed surfaces and edges of the wood after cutting it into an amorphous shape. We used polyurethane to coat the backs and sides – several coats, sanding between each coat. This was supposed to inhibit moisture from saturating the panel.

After the polyurethane dried, we painted those surfaces with blue enamel. We used thinset mortar to set the tile and to grout. We used tile sealer over the grout.

The piece survived the bumpy truck-ride over south Jersey back-roads to Oceanville unscathed. Noyes director Mike Cagno and I installed the panel in the sculpture garden just in time to be exposed to a nasty thunderstorm that was rolling through the area.

A week later we attended the opening reception at the Noyes, and the piece looked superb. Spotlights in the garden reflected off of the mirrored tile and added mystery and depth to the installation. We were happy.

The mural did not last the year or so that we had anticipated. Within a few weeks of torrential downpours and humid weather the tiles began delaminating from the board in sheets. The mortar did its job and held the tiles together. The problem is that the wood swelled just enough to break the hold of the mosaic. When we implore you that wood is not to be used for an outdoor project, it is solid advice.

It doesn't matter how many coats of paint or polyurethane you apply, wood will warp when the humidity changes and your best laid plans will end up a pile of rubble beneath a blank wood surface.

INSTALLATIONS FROM START TO FINISH

Laying out the patterns. It doesn't look like much right now. The union tile setters were scratching their heads wondering what we were doing!

Laying out the design

Now we come to the heart of the book, the reason you parted with your hard-earned money to acquire this bound collection of paper. For your part, you have by now acquired the tools and purchased the supplies you will need for your project. You are ready to begin. For this section we will guide you from beginning to end on the installation of a large-scale exterior mural. I will include special notes in cases where procedures or materials will deviate for interior projects.

Think of the wall as a blank canvas, and using your permanent marker or chalk sketch out the rough patterns of the mural. This process is not to be taken lightly; the key to success is all in the prep work. If you slack off on the preparation it will be glaringly apparent in the finished product.

We each have our own strengths, and our own weaknesses. When submitting proposals for jobs, I do the computer work, putting together what required documentation is needed, creating Power Point presentations, and burning CD's with images. Liz is good at imagining designs, and putting them onto paper. If I have ideas, I generally tell Liz and she translates it onto paper.

The completed mural as seen in the evening with spotlights. This mural was done by Liz and carl, with the assistance of two apprentices over the course of eight weeks.

For this project I will skip the sordid details of endless meetings and revisions, and fast-forward to the installation. We had the conceptual drawings approved by committee, as the installation process of this project commenced. Using cheap dollar store versions of a broad point Sharpie, Liz drew outlines based on the sketches on the concrete block wall.

The contractors on the project had prepped the wall according to our specs. The concrete block wall had been capped, and the top, sides and rear had been painted with a sealer to prevent moisture from seeping through. No sealer was applied to the surface to be tiled.

This design relied extensively on the lines created by mirror. The mirror reflects the surroundings, and causes the mural to come to life as you walk by. The mirror was applied following the drawn lines, creating divisions that would frame each field of color.

HOW TO MIX MORTAR

Into a large plastic bucket add a couple inches of cold water. Do not use warm or hot water, as this will cause the mortar to set more rapidly.

Use enough mortar to fill a quart container and dump it into the water.

Mix the mortar with a paddle, gradually add more cool water until the mix is sticky wet, but firm.

You don't want gravy. We actually want the mortar to be a little firmer than it would be for grouting. We want the tiles to stick to the surface and not slide down.

Mix thoroughly until the mix is creamy smooth with no lumps. After you mix, let the thinset rest for about 10 minutes. It will start to stiffen-up and get thick. Now mix again, it will loosen up and be ready for use.

For this project we used thinset mortar mixed with an acrylic "milk" which helps add a waterproof barrier between the tile and the wall surface as our adhesive. You can purchase thinset that already has the additive. To mix, use a clean 5-gallon bucket. Add a couple inches of cold water. Do not use warm or hot water, as this will cause the mortar to set more rapidly.

You will want to mix smaller quantities than you would for tiling a wall or floor

You can use acrylic tile mastic for many interior projects. You do not want to use mastic for tiles that will be on a floor and are larger than 6x6 inches, or that will be in an underwater environment.

The benefit of mastic is that there is no mixing involved.

simply because the process of laying out the designs adds quite a bit of time as opposed to tiling a floor. If you are a seasoned tile or terrazzo setter, many of the processes will run counter to your instincts.

For our purposes we begin with enough mortar to fill a quart container and dump it into the water. Mix the mortar with a paddle, gradually add more cool water until the mix is sticky wet, but firm. You don't want gravy. We actually want the mortar to be a little firmer than it would be for grouting. We want the tiles to stick to the surface and not slide down.

SAFETY TIP!
Wear latex or vinyl gloves when mixing and applying mortar. Mortar contains lime and that will wreak havoc on your hands. If you have any cuts, ouch!

When working with mortar or grout, **never, ever** clean your tools or buckets in the kitchen sink! The mortar might seem to wash down easily, but it WILL harden. If you think those hair clogs are hard to remove, Draino will not touch this stuff! Always clean outside using a garden hose.

Student mural at The Glasstown Plaza, Millville, NJ

Some people prefer using an electric stirrer. Use the paddle, you get a good feeling of the consistency of the mortar, you build muscle, and what are you anyway, a man or a mouse?

Mix thoroughly until the mix is creamy smooth with no lumps. Think Cream of Wheat! After you mix, let the thinset rest for about 10 minutes. It will start to stiffen-up and get thick. Now mix again, it will loosen up and be ready for use. The process of allowing the thinset to rest between the initial mixing and second missing is called slaking. Slaking will extend the working life of the mortar. If the batch starts to thicken as the job progresses, just remix it and it will loosen up. Never add more water to a mixed batch.

If you were working on an interior mural, instead of mortar you would use standard tile mastic. The benefit of mastic is that there is no mixing required. You just open the container and begin sticking tile! For interior projects you can use wood as a sub-surface, but we still discourage it. We recommend concrete board or wall board. Just make sure there is no "give" in the surface. The surface must be solid and secure.

"Imagine" 5' x5', Gloucester County Health Dept, Sewell, NJ

"Phases" - the mural that started everything. "AtlantiCare Regional Medical Center, Center for Childbirth, Pomona, NJ

41

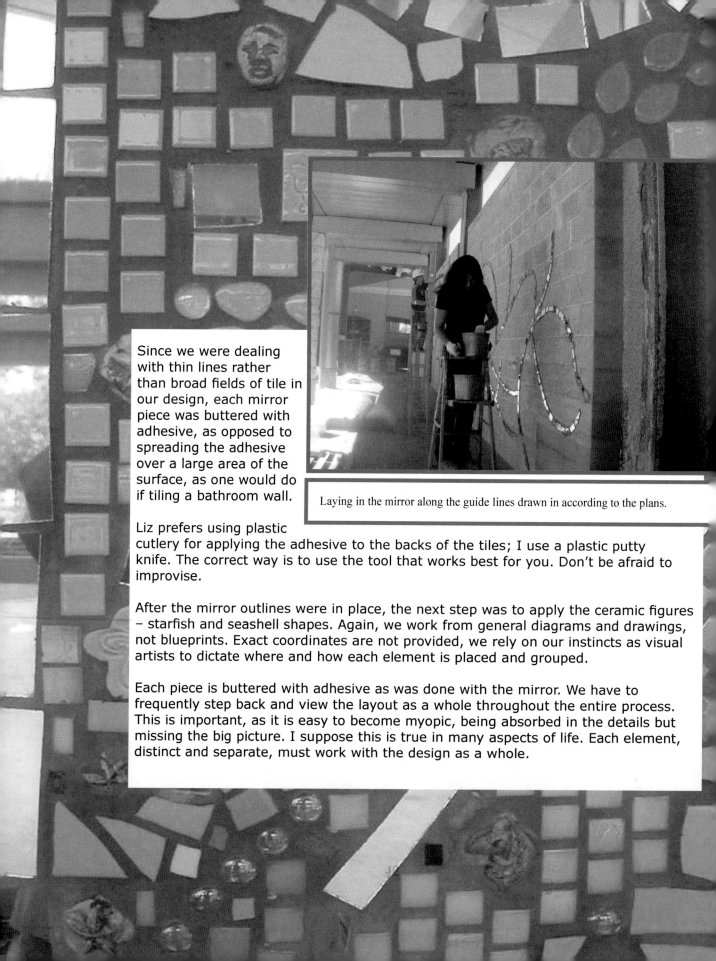

Since we were dealing with thin lines rather than broad fields of tile in our design, each mirror piece was buttered with adhesive, as opposed to spreading the adhesive over a large area of the surface, as one would do if tiling a bathroom wall.

Laying in the mirror along the guide lines drawn in according to the plans.

Liz prefers using plastic cutlery for applying the adhesive to the backs of the tiles; I use a plastic putty knife. The correct way is to use the tool that works best for you. Don't be afraid to improvise.

After the mirror outlines were in place, the next step was to apply the ceramic figures – starfish and seashell shapes. Again, we work from general diagrams and drawings, not blueprints. Exact coordinates are not provided, we rely on our instincts as visual artists to dictate where and how each element is placed and grouped.

Each piece is buttered with adhesive as was done with the mirror. We have to frequently step back and view the layout as a whole throughout the entire process. This is important, as it is easy to become myopic, being absorbed in the details but missing the big picture. I suppose this is true in many aspects of life. Each element, distinct and separate, must work with the design as a whole.

FILLING IN THE BLANKS

Now that the general design has been defined, we get to fill in the blanks. This is the fun part of the process. We get to decide whether we want to go with rectangular pieces, or triangular, or squares. Do we want a sunburst effect, or long rolling curves? We allow our creative juices to flow, adding tile, stepping back, making minor adjustments and adding more tiles.

For this project, the overall effect that Liz desired was that of rolling waves. This dictated the tile and glass color as well as the orientation of the tiles. The stained glass was cut into elongated rectangular shapes. Fields were laid out, and we made sure that we worked on the wall as a whole, doing a section on the top left, then going to the bottom right, then to the middle perhaps.

A mistake that you want to avoid is attempting to lay tile left to right. You are not writing a novel, you are creating a visual work of art, and the secret is to work on it as a whole. Fill in one area and jump across to another, starting with large pieces and going smaller. Don't worry about the small gaps yet. Your purpose now is to fill in the broad canvas; we will work on the details later.

Our stained glass was laid in sweeping flowing arcs and swirls. We used ceramic tile, broken into random shapes and sizes for solid fields of blue, white and green. The trick to laying these tiles, as they will not fit into any predetermined pattern, is to make sure you have a border to one side of the field. You lay tile edge to edge along that border. You then find two edges that are perpendicular, and continue filling in. You are not creating patterns, but relying on the randomness of the pieces to fill in an expanse. Do not over-analyze.

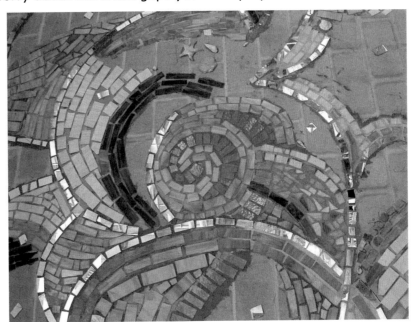

Don't let empty spaces disturb you. Just keep filling in, and filling in. Start large and work down to smaller tile.

43

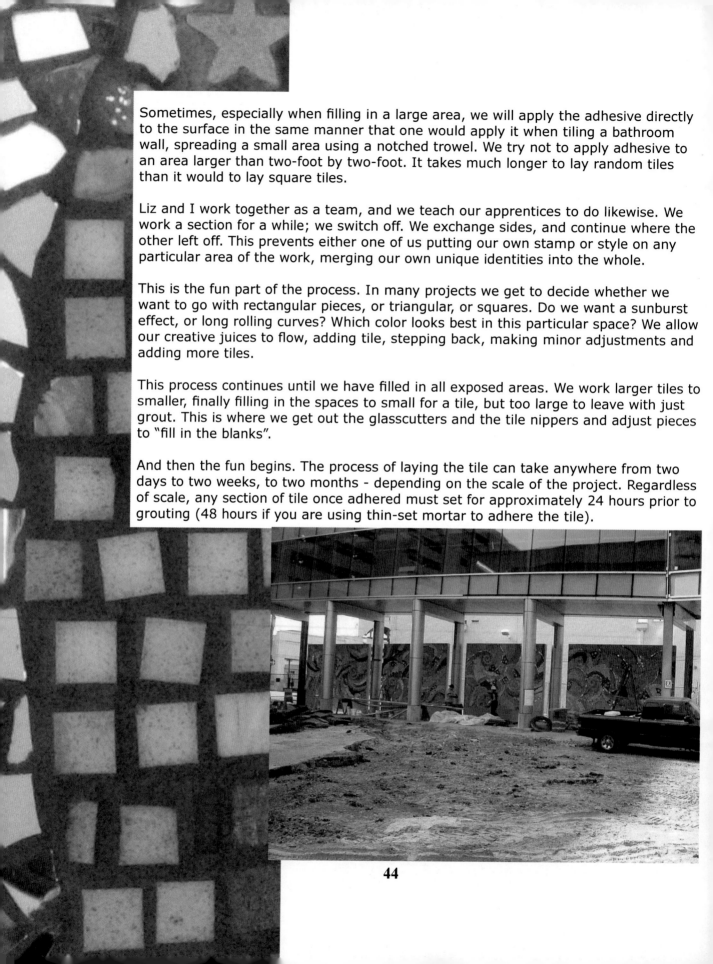

Sometimes, especially when filling in a large area, we will apply the adhesive directly to the surface in the same manner that one would apply it when tiling a bathroom wall, spreading a small area using a notched trowel. We try not to apply adhesive to an area larger than two-foot by two-foot. It takes much longer to lay random tiles than it would to lay square tiles.

Liz and I work together as a team, and we teach our apprentices to do likewise. We work a section for a while; we switch off. We exchange sides, and continue where the other left off. This prevents either one of us putting our own stamp or style on any particular area of the work, merging our own unique identities into the whole.

This is the fun part of the process. In many projects we get to decide whether we want to go with rectangular pieces, or triangular, or squares. Do we want a sunburst effect, or long rolling curves? Which color looks best in this particular space? We allow our creative juices to flow, adding tile, stepping back, making minor adjustments and adding more tiles.

This process continues until we have filled in all exposed areas. We work larger tiles to smaller, finally filling in the spaces to small for a tile, but too large to leave with just grout. This is where we get out the glasscutters and the tile nippers and adjust pieces to "fill in the blanks".

And then the fun begins. The process of laying the tile can take anywhere from two days to two weeks, to two months - depending on the scale of the project. Regardless of scale, any section of tile once adhered must set for approximately 24 hours prior to grouting (48 hours if you are using thin-set mortar to adhere the tile).

GROUTING

After a section has thoroughly dried, the process of grouting may begin. Before grouting, we do a once over inspection of the mural, scraping excess adhesive that might be thicker than the thickness of the tile. A single edge razor blade works well to clean adhesive and mortar from the surfaces of the tile. A metal-blade putty knife will also suffice.

We are ready to begin grouting, and for our exterior mural we will use thinset mortar as grout. We now mix mortar in the method prescribed previously. The difference is the mortar should be a little bit looser so that it can be worked into the spaces between tiles. Again, it should not be so thin that it runs down the wall, but we do not want gaps or space under the surface. You will want to mix these batches in larger quantities than you would when using it as an adhesive.

The mural does not need to be finished to begin grouting. As long as the adhesive process has been given 48 hours to dry, you can begin slectively grouting finished areas, as we did here.

The grout is what holds the entire mural into place, and when dry it will take a chisel and a lot of muscle and sweat to remove any pieces. The benefit of using thinset for both adhesive and grout for an outside installation is that the finished work is all but impervious to weather. It is not going anywhere without the use of a sledgehammer.

MiXiNg GRoUT

Mixing grout is very similar to the process of mixing thinset mortar, except that you can ignore the slaking process.

Always use sanded grout. Sanded grout is stronger than non-sanded grout, and is desgined for the wider gaps that you have with mosaics.

Just like mixing mortar, into a bit of water add the grout.

Adding the grout to the water rather than vice versa prevents dry areas of unmoistened mix at the bottom of the container.

Mix thoroughly, making sure to work out any clumps.

We are going for the consistency of thick cream of wheat, thick enough so that it doesn't run, but thin enough to work into the gaps between tiles.

Custom Colored Grout

Most store-bought grout comes in a limited, and to some, boring color selection. You can buy white grout. You can buy beige, and you can buy a different shade of beige, and you can buy a darker shade of beige. You can get many shades of gray.

But what do you do when your project just screams for bold colors? You mix your own color!

Now take note - if you are working on a very large projects, it will be next to impossible to mix the same shade and hue consistently. You will have to take pains to measure exact amounts of colorant with exact amounts of grout with exact amounts of water to achieve seamless color throughout.

Liz and I use standard acrylic paint, either from the tube or bottle to mix custom colors. The color will fade in direct sunlight, but is otherwise pretty much permanent even for exterior installations.

Mosaic supply stores sell highly concentrated powder pigment, which is another option. You simply mix the powder into the grout until you achieve the shade you want. Remember that most grout will dry a shade or so lighter than it appears when wet.

For an interior project we will use sanded grout. If you don't know what you are looking for, it is easy to become overwhelmed by the choices and selections of grout.

Always use sanded grout. Unsanded grout gives a smooth grout line, but it is intended for tiles with joints less than 1/16 inch wide, and intended only for use on walls, not floors. Mosaic installations typically have uneven and large joint gaps. Sanded grout is easier to clean from porous or semi-porous tiles, and also stronger than unsanded. As a novice mosaicist, Liz once used pre-colored, black, unsanded grout for a garden pot. We can only describe the experience as having been like trying to remove tar when time came to clean off the pot.

If you are going with a colored grout, whether using grout or mortar, use a standard factory color. It is nearly impossible to match your own custom colors from batch to batch. Remember – always mix darker than you want the color to be – it lightens as it dries. When doing exterior public work, we try to use a standard color. That way, if there is ever any repair work to be done, it will be seamless. Also - no matter what pigment you use - COLOR FADES from the UV rays of the sun.

For large projects, buy more than enough grout to ensure that you will have it on hand to complete the project. You can always return any extra bags. If you are using colored grout, make sure all bags are from the same lot number. You don't want obvious changes in color, and similar colors from the same manufacturer will have slight variations from lot to lot.

Mix grout according to directions. It is very similar to the process of mixing thinset mortar, except that you can ignore the slaking process. You do not want it watery, it has to stick like my Cream of Wheat, and not slide out with the pull of gravity.

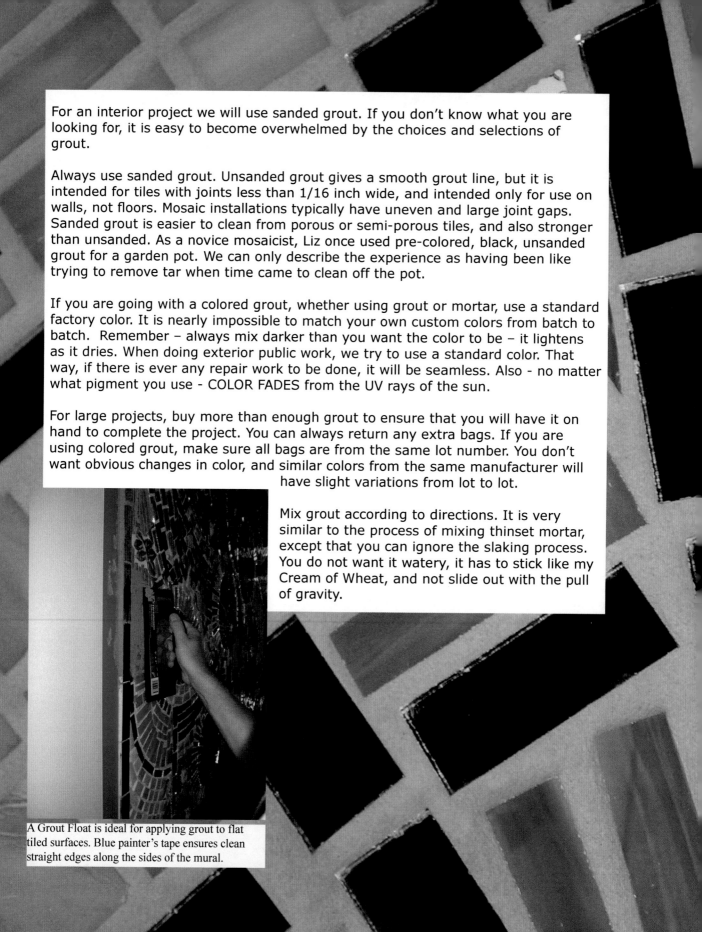

A Grout Float is ideal for applying grout to flat tiled surfaces. Blue painter's tape ensures clean straight edges along the sides of the mural.

Apply the grout in small areas, no larger than about four-foot square. As mentioned earlier that I prefer using a grout float, and Liz uses a sponge. For a sponge, Liz uses the large sponges you will find in the automotive department for washing your car.

With either method, you use your tool of choice to push the grout in between all tiles and objects, making sure to leave no gaps or air pockets. Any gap will trap moisture and compromise the installation.

After all the gaps are filled with grout, scrape the excess off with the edge of the float; or using your sponge or soft rag, wipe off gently careful not to gouge the gaps. Using dry soft rags, such as cotton tee shirts, old washcloths, or old sweatshirts that you no longer use because you are too lazy to go jogging anymore, gently wipe the surface of the tiles.

With every pass, you will see as more and more of the haze comes off. As the grout dries, you can use more pressure, making sure to clean the grout off of the entire surface of the tiles. You want to have sharp corners and edges.

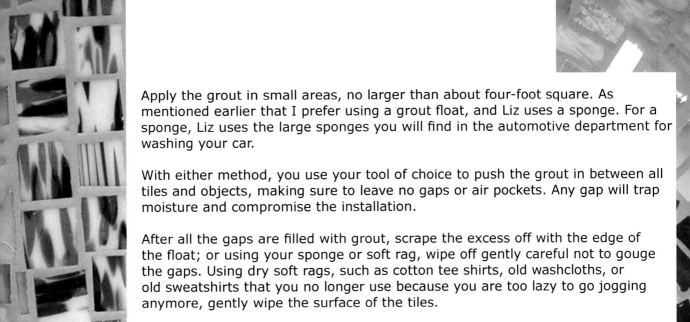

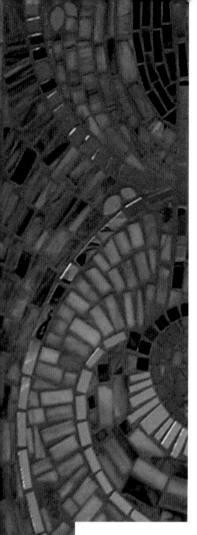

The fun process of grouting involves a lot of wiping, you push the grout in to fill all of the gaps, and then you wipe, wipe, wipe.

If you have ever watched home improvement shows on the TV, you might have heard them advise to use damp cloths for this cleaning process. DO NOT DO THAT! This is not a bathroom shower stall. This is not a kitchen countertop. This is a mosaic mural; the gaps are much wider than your typical home tile job. Water will serve only to smear an ugly haze over the tiles you are trying to polish.

Just keep using fresh sides of your endless supply of rags, you did bring a bundle, didn't you? Continue wiping with clean rags, shake the excess dried grout off frequently, and keep polishing like the Karate Kid! Wax on, wax off.

Start a four-foot square section; wipe the wet stuff off. Apply grout to another four-foot square section, as that begins to dry go back to the first. Clean the first some more. Go to the second section, clean it some more; begin a third. Go back to the first and wipe clean, wipe more on the second, on so on. This is a good time to practice your Zen meditation.

There you have it. With these skills and an artistic imagination the sky is the limit. Well, maybe not the sky, but any solid wall will suffice.

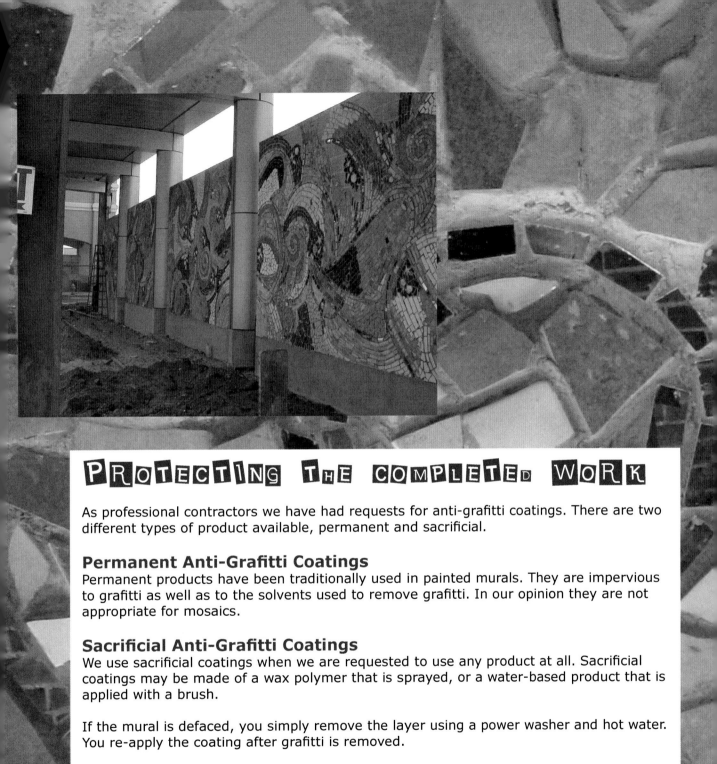

PROTECTING THE COMPLETED WORK

As professional contractors we have had requests for anti-grafitti coatings. There are two different types of product available, permanent and sacrificial.

Permanent Anti-Grafitti Coatings
Permanent products have been traditionally used in painted murals. They are impervious to grafitti as well as to the solvents used to remove grafitti. In our opinion they are not appropriate for mosaics.

Sacrificial Anti-Grafitti Coatings
We use sacrificial coatings when we are requested to use any product at all. Sacrificial coatings may be made of a wax polymer that is sprayed, or a water-based product that is applied with a brush.

If the mural is defaced, you simply remove the layer using a power washer and hot water. You re-apply the coating after grafitti is removed.

The limitations of these products is that they can be compromised if they are abraded.

SHOULD YOU USE AN ANTI-GRAFITTI COATING?

While an anti-grafitti coating will make clean-up of a defaced mural a bit easier, there are drawbacks.

The coating that we use must be applied with a brush, and leaves a clear film that is apparent on mirror. It also costs $50 a gallon, and shipping is expensive.

If grafitti is going to be an ongoing problem you might want to seriously consider using one of these products. However, if your mural is primarily ceramic tile and glass, spray paint is fairly easily cleaned from these materials. A razor blade will easily remove the spray, and solvents will remove marker.

Paint will absorb into the grout, but it is a simple matter to use a triangular scraper to remove the discolored grout. Simply re-grout those areas.

"Gaia", part of the "Earth Trilogy" by Liz Nicklus

HOW IT BECAME A BUSINESS

We had completed our first project as a team. We both fell comfortably into our unique roles. Liz is great at developing the rough design concepts and putting them on paper; I am more the organizer. I read through the prospectus and develop the presentations, and anything else on the computer end. I do the heavy lifting and she watches me.

We had completed the project at the senior center and were involved in talks with a developer for potential jobs on the West Coast and elsewhere. As in any business that requires salesmanship, you follow all leads. We decided at this juncture to treat it as a business.

From that moment on we began publicizing ourselves at every chance. We respond to every prospectus for public and corporate art if we see a potential fit. We teach workshops of pique assiette mosaic. And from these ventures was born this book.

We continue to experiment with new methods and materials. No table is safe in our house. Our back yard is becoming populated with pebble-mosaic stepping stones. Cement statuary and flowerpots get covered with tile and left in the rain and snow to see how long they take to self-destruct.

It is our sincere hope that the guidelines we have provided in this manual will start you on your way to a rewarding new venture. Whether you are looking to create an artsy backsplash in your kitchen or mosaic the side of a building, the techniques and tips we presented will give you the courage you need to tackle the project. It is not rocket science – just common sense, ingenuity, hard work, and the eye of an artist!

Appendix 1

Resources

Retailers and Wholesalers:
Mullica Hill Art Glass (mysite.verizon.net/bizt3vzu) for stained glass.
> This is our local south Jersey glass supplier. They carry a large supply of stained glass, and are happy to accommodate large orders. Great customer service!

Delphi Glass (www.delphiglass.com) for stained glass.

Mosaic Source (www.mosaicsource.com) for mosaic tiles.
Mosaic Art Supply (www.mosaicartsupply.com) for mosaic tiles and supplies.
Mosaic Mercantile (mosaicmercantile.com) for mosaic tiles and supplies.

Your local home improvement and hardware stores are a great source for ceramic tile, thinset, grout, mastic, tools and other supplies:
Home Depot (www.homedepot.com)
Lowes (www.Lowes.com)
Ace Hardware (www.acehardware.com)

Arts and crafts supply stores, they carry a many mosaic supplies:
Michaels (www.michaels.com)
A. C. Moore (www.acmoore.com)

Online arts and crafts suppliers
Dick Blick (www.dickblick.com)

Products:
Wedi® Board concrete backer board. Wedi® Board is good for any installation that will see dampness or wetness.

Laticrete® 9237 Waterproof Membrane is a perfect sealer for concrete walls, and especially useful for ground applications, if you are doing a walkway.

Sacrificial Coating SC-1 by Prosoco (www.prosoco.com)
GPC-103 Sacrificial Coating by SEI (www.seichemical.com)

Mosaic Art Concentrated Colorant (www.diamondtechcrafts.com)

Mosaic Mural Check List

- ☐ Mastic (Indoor)
- ☐ Sanded Grout (Indoor)
- ☐ Thin Set Mortar (Outdoor)
- ☐ Wide Masking Tape
- ☐ Regular Masking Tape
- ☐ Plastic Drop Cloths
- ☐ Canvas Drop Cloth
- ☐ Pre-taped Plastic Drop Cloth
- ☐ Glass Cutters
- ☐ Cutting Oil
- ☐ Safety Glasses
- ☐ Glass Running Pliers
- ☐ Tile Nippers
- ☐ Tile Cutters
- ☐ Measuring Tape
- ☐ Level
- ☐ Permanent Marker or Chalk
- ☐ Latex or Vinyl Gloves
- ☐ Plastic Buckets – 5-Gallon
- ☐ Plastic Buckets – 1-Quart
- ☐ Putty Knives
- ☐ Notched Trowel
- ☐ Sponges
- ☐ Grout Floats
- ☐ Paper Plates
- ☐ Plastic Knives
- ☐ Rags
- ☐ First Aid Kit
- ☐ Sun Block

If you are working outside, don't forget to pack the sun block.

ABOUT THE AUTHORS

Independent Artist Studios is Liz Nicklus and Carl B. Johnson. We are members of the Society of American Mosaic Artists.

Liz Nicklus

Liz Nicklus is an award winning mosaic and mixed media artist who resides in Millville,

N.J. She began her artistic career as a traditional oil painter and watercolorist, but later became captivated by the textural possibilities inherent in the art of mosaics. Her work in mosaics, mixed media and assemblage compliment each other in style and content. It often involves the use of non-traditional materials, and she enjoys surprising viewers by pushing the limits of the media she chooses. Her mosaic installations consist of intricate patterns unified by complex color relationships.

Nicklus studied at Stockton State College, the Ridgewood School of Art, Fleisher Art Memorial, with Pat Witt at The Barn Studio of Art in Millville, and with Philadelphia mosaic artist Isaiah Zagar. She was Discover New Jersey Arts featured artist in April 2004. She is past chair and one of the founding members of the Riverfront Renaissance Center for the Arts in Millville, and is on the Board of Directors of the DaVinci Art Alliance in Philadelphia. Together with Millville artist Carl B. Johnson, she is a partner in the Independent Artist Studios. She currently teaches mixed media and mosaics throughout Philadelphia and southern New Jersey, and has been a guest instructor at the Studios of Key West in Florida. She also works as an independent curator, and has hosted many ground-breaking shows within Millville's fledgling arts district. Her own work can be seen in public and private collections throughout the world.

Carl B. Johnson

Carl B. Johnson has been
called a "twisted Hopper"
and dubbed "outlaw artist"
by friend and renowned poet,
walt Christopher stickney.
He has exhibited extensively
throughout the southern
New Jersey & Philadelphia
region. His work resides in
private collections throughout
the United States. A representational painter, Carl obscures the lines between Abstract
Expressionism and Contemporary Impressionism creating a style that is truly unique. His
most recent works involve the artist's observations of disappearing faces and scenes in
his community.

Carl is partner with Liz Nicklus in the Independent Artist Studios, creating large-scale
public mosaic mural installations, such as the 10 by 65-foot exterior installation the
Atlantic Regional Medical Center in Atlantic City, NJ.

Carl has served as an officer on the board of directors of the Riverfront Renaissance
Center for the Arts for the first few years of its development, and currently sits on the
board of directors of Da Vinci Art Alliance in Philadelphia. He is a founding member
of the Glasstown Nine, a painting group comprised of Cumberland County artists. He
publishes a regional arts newspaper, "INFERNO".

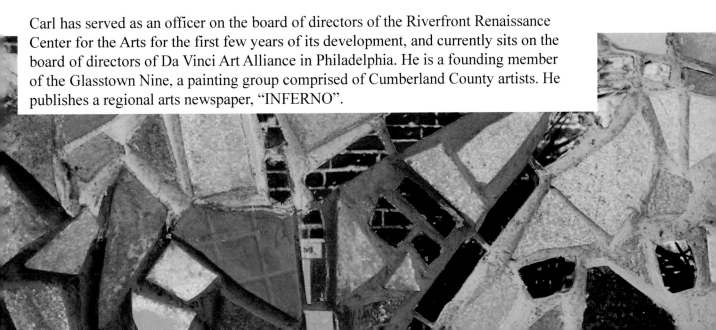

Independent Artist Studios

Independent Artist Studios is currently located in the renowned arts district of Millville, in the heart of south Jersey. IAS has earned a reputation of creating and installing quality and innovative public and corporate art. Our installations are located in hospitals, senior housing complexes, public buildings and parks, and colleges.

No job is too big; more important - no job is too small. Are you looking for that one-of-a-kind kitchen backsplash? A unique floor treatment? Accents for your fishpond or garden walk? Your imagination is your only limitation.

We are happy to collaborate with your designer or architect to ensure that our overall design compliments your project. We will coordinate with your contractors and project managers in scheduling.

Contact Us at!

IndependentArtistStudios.com

Carl B. Johnson - webmaster@wuli.com

Liz Nicklus - LizNicklus@gmail.com

HOW TO GET THE BIG JOBS

Perhaps you bought this book with the intention of learning how to do large-scale mosiacs for a personal project and now you want to expand your scope, and do some jobs professionally. Where to begin?

One source is SAMA, the Society of Mosaic Artists (www.americanmosaics.org). Membership is relatively inexpensive (and a tax write-off). They have a regular newsletter and an extensive website full of resources for professional mosaic artists.

Another website of note is CAFE (www.callforentry.org). CAFE is free to join, and provides calls for entry country-wide. Many of the calls for entry can be completed online using their website.

Many cities and states have a "percent for arts" - a percentage of new construction that is allocated for public art. The secret is to apply for any RFP (request for proposal) that you are qualified for. This process can be a full time job in itself; expect ten rejections before you get one acceptance letter. But one job can pay off big time.

The trick with RFP's is to read them carefully, and follow the instructions to a "t".
The committees get hundreds upon hundreds of applicants, and sort through applications ruthlessly, tossing any that are out of compliance without even considering the artist, simply to reduce the workload.

It takes patience, perserverence, and sometimes a bit dumb luck. Once you get your foot in the door, every new job becomes easier.

Liz Nicklus and Carl B. Johnson in Cape May New Jersey, waiting in line for the Saturday Afternoon Jam at the Cape May Jazz Festival.

MOSAIC WORKSHOPS

We are available to teach mosaic workshops to any skill level. Our workshops are personalized to your students skill levels. We teach beginners as well as those with experience.

Learn the basics of the direct method of pique assiette mosaics, or "shard art". A typical workshop consists of two full days. The student will learn about substrates, materials, cutting, nipping, adhesives, design and many other tricks of the trade from a professional mosaic artist.

First, they will observe a demonstration, then go on to work on an individual project of their choice. Students will supply their own tools and materials.

At the end of the workshop, each student will leave with a finished piece of his or her own design and will have all the knowledge necessary to continue to create additional projects.

We also give apprenticeships to qualified students for large-scale installations. For more information, please visit our website at www.independentartiststudios.com.

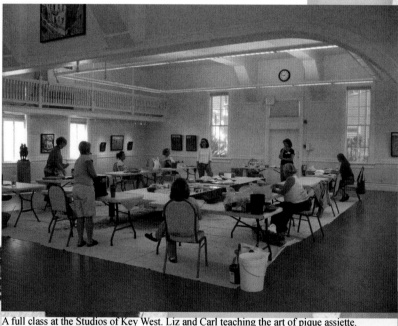

A full class at the Studios of Key West. Liz and Carl teaching the art of pique assiette.

We limit class size to ensure one-on-one instruction.

Class participants learn how to mix custom colors, and proper techniques of every step of mosaic creation. It is a simple matter to take these lessons and apply them to projects of any size or scope.

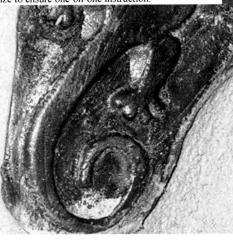

At the end of the class every student will have created a project of their choosing.

Other Books Available on the INFERNO Label

Bar Exam - Musings from the Bar Stool
by Carl B. Johnson
Bar Exam is a full color collection of Carl's paintings of the disappearing neighborhood tavern, and his musings of life on a bar stool. The articles in this book initially appeared in the underground newspaper, INFERNO.

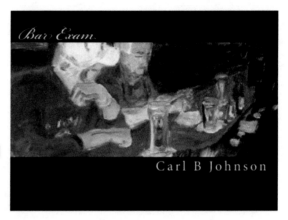

Price - $12.00
ISBN: 144955654X
Buy direct at: www.createspace.com/3405229

Mo Knows
by Mo Pagano
Mo Knows art. Mo penned a column for INFERNO from its inception concerning everything from art to boxing to jazz to NYC in the 1950's. Full color reproductions of Mo's paintings and much more!
Price - $12.00
ISBN: 1450503675
Buy direct at: www.createspace.com/3422480

INFERNO - Burning the Bridges Behind Us
The Bad Economy Edition
INFERNO Newspaper was an underground arts newspaper that had a seven year run. This book has the best of INFERNO and brand new commentary and articles by the original band of contributors. 222 pages.
Price - $19.99
ISBN: 1451531974
Buy direct at: www.createspace.com/3437929

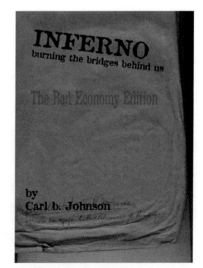

Made in the USA
Middletown, DE
04 September 2020